NICHOLAS II
THE IMPERIAL FAMILY

ABRIS PUBLISHERS

ST PETERSBURG • PETERHOF

2004

For the 300th Anniversary of Peterhof
1705–2005

Authors of the concept of this book: **Vadim Znamenov**,
Director General of the Peterhof Museum Complex

Sergei Mironenko,
Director of the State Archive of the Russian Federation, Doctor of History

Olga Barkovets

The preparation of the present Almanac has been contributed by

the Peterhof Museum Complex:
Nina Vernova, scholarly consultant
Valentina Tenikhina, author of the essay "The Lower Dacha"
compilers of notes on the plates:
Tatyana Igumnova, Marina Kaznakova,
Tamara Nosovich, Valentina Tenikhina,
Marina Trubanovskaya, Nina Vernova

the State Archive of the Russian Federation:
Yelena Chirkova, head of the group
Olga Barkovets, author of the essay "OTMA Plus Alexis"
Anastasia Atapina, Larisa Kriachkova,
Igor Tikhonov, Victoria Zakirova, Irina Zasypkina

the Museum of Artillery, Engineering Troops and Signal Corps:
Piotr Goregliad

Abris Publishers express gratitude for the lent material to:
the Peterhof Museum Complex
the State Archive of the Russian Federation, Moscow
the State Hermitage, St Petersburg
the Museum of Artillery, Engineering Troops and Signal Corps, St Petersburg

Almanac: **Treasures of Russia** *Issue 62*

Texts by Olga Barkovets and Valentina Tenikhina
Edited by Olga Akbulatova
Translated from the Russian by Valery Fateyev
Designed by Alexander Pompeyev
Photographs by Nikolai Alexeyev, Alexander Ivanov and Alexander Pompeyev

Printed in Finland
Тираж 1000. Цена договорная
№ П2462 в СЗРУ Госкомпечати РФ от 30.04.97
ISBN 5-88810-013-7

Abris Publishers – tel. (812) 934-74-95, 951-35-50, e-mail: pompeev@mail.convey.ru

OTMA Plus Alexis

They liked to write letters and usually signed them with their common signature OTMA, the acronym of Olga, Tatyana, Marie and Anastasia. The four daughters of Emperor Nicholas II and the Heir Alexis shared the terrible lot of their parents. Their only fault in the eyes of their executioners was their royal origin.

They entered this world just for a moment — the eldest daughter was twenty-two when she died, and the youngest was merely seventeen… Alexis would be fourteen in a half of month.

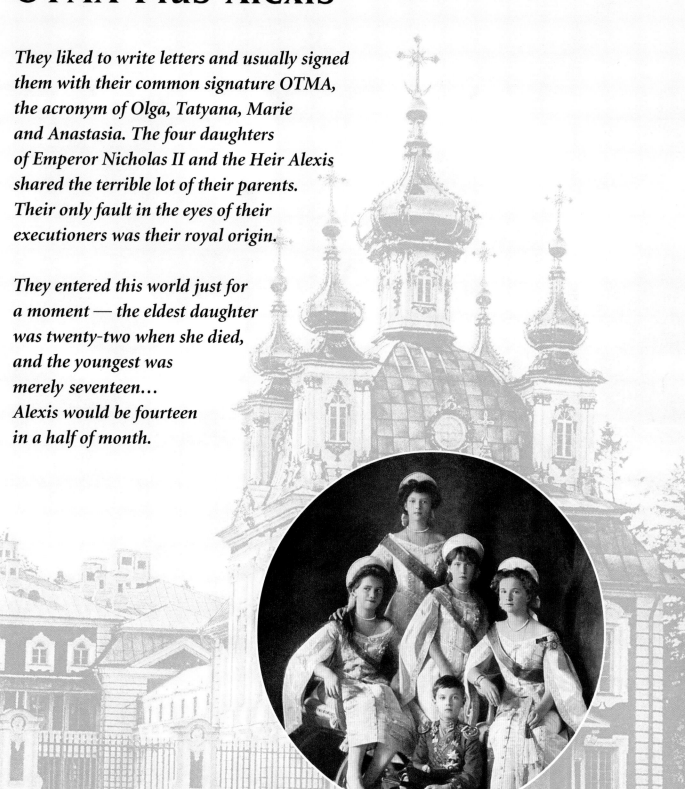

The wedding of Emperor Nicholas II and Alice or Alix, the Princess of Hesse, took place in November 1894, a month after the bride had adopted the Orthodox religion under the name of Alexandra Feodorovna. The bride came to St Petersburg, as bitter tongues said, following the coffin of Emperor Alexander III. The wedding was modest, unlike a royal one, because it was celebrated amidst a general mourning for the deceased Tsar.

A year after the wedding the first daughter was born to the imperial couple and named Olga. On 3 November 1895 Nicholas II wrote in his *Diary*: "Tsarskoye Selo… A day I will remember for ever, during which I suffered a very great deal. Labour pains that did not let my dear Alix to sleep began as early as one o'clock after the midnight. She stayed in bed all day long afflicted with pain — poor thing! I could not stand watching her. At about two o'clock in the morning dear Mama [Dowager Empress Marie Feodorovna] arrived from Gatchina; she, Ella and I were by Alex's bedside the whole time. At nine sharp we heard a child squealing, and all of us felt relieved".[1]

This anxiety about the wife's health and unskilled care of the young father are very touching. "Of course I was present for our daughter's bath. She is a big baby weighing 10 pounds and measuring 55 centimeters. I can hardly believe it's really our child! God what happiness!"[2] The Empress decided to start feeding the baby herself. In a week after the daughter's birth the Emperor wrote to the wife's grandmother, Queen Victoria of England: "She finds such a pleasure in nursing our sweet baby herself. For my part I consider it the most natural thing a mother can do and I think the example an excellent one!… The name of Olga we chose as it has already been several times in our family and is an ancient Russian name. You don't know, dearest Grandmama, the state of what happiness I am in. It seems so strange to be a father."[3]

During the first anniversary of the parents' wedding, on 14 November, the ceremony of the newly born girl's baptism took place.

**The future Emperor Nicholas II with his bride Alice of Hesse.
Coburg. 1894. State Archive of the Russian Federation**

[1] *Dnevniki imperatora Nikolaya II*, Moscow, 1991, p. 111.
[2] *Idem*, p. 111. Entry of 4 November.
[3] State Archive of the Russian Federation, fund 601, l. 1. No 1111.

*Laurits Regner Tuxen
(1853–1927). The Wedding
of Emperor Nicholas II and
Empress Alexandra Feodorovna.
1895. The Hermitage,
St Petersburg*

Olga was, to use popular expression, "father's daughter". She inherited his form of the eyes, the slightly snub "Romanov" nose and outstanding physical fitness. Over the years the girl shaped a strong, firm character, which sometimes accounted for her strikingly stubborn behaviour, with which Olga's mother vainly tried to struggle. In 1909 Empress Alexandra Feodorovna instructed her eldest daughter: "Try to be an example of what a good little obedient girlie ought to be. You are the eldest and must show the others how to behave. Learn to make others happy, think of yourself last of all. Be gentle and kind, never rough nor rude. In manners as well as in speech

БОЖIЕЮ МИЛОСТIЮ

МЫ, НИКОЛАЙ ВТОРЫЙ,

ИМПЕРАТОРЪ И САМОДЕРЖЕЦЪ

ВСЕРОССIЙСКIЙ,

ЦАРЬ ПОЛЬСКIЙ, ВЕЛИКIЙ КНЯЗЬ ФИНЛЯНДСКIЙ.

И ПРОЧАЯ, И ПРОЧАЯ, И ПРОЧАЯ.

Объявляемъ всѣмъ НАШИМЪ вѣрноподданнымъ:

Въ 3-й день сего Ноября Любезнѣйшая Супруга НАША ГОСУДАРЫНЯ ИМПЕ-РАТРИЦА АЛЕКСАНДРА ѲЕОДОРОВНА благополучно разрѣшилась отъ бремени рожде-ніемъ НАМЪ Дочери, нареченной Ольгою.

Таковое ИМПЕРАТОРСКАГО Дома НАШЕГО приращеніе пріемля новымъ ознамено-ваніемъ благодати Божіей, на НАСЪ и Имперію НАШУ изливаемой, возвѣщаемъ о семъ радостномъ событіи вѣрнымъ НАШИМЪ подданнымъ и вмѣстѣ съ ними возносимъ къ Всевышнему горячія молитвы о благополучномъ возрастаніи и преуспѣяніи Новорожденной.

ПОВЕЛѢВАЕМЪ писать и именовать, во всѣхъ дѣлахъ, гдѣ приличествуетъ, Лю-безнѣйшую НАШУ Дочь, Великую Княжну Ольгу Николаевну Ея Импе-РАТОРСКИМЪ Высочествомъ.

Данъ въ Царскомъ Селѣ, въ 3-й день Ноября, въ лѣто отъ Рождества Христова тысяча восемьсотъ девяносто пятое, Царствованія же НАШЕГО во второе.

На подлинномъ Собственною ЕГО ИМПЕРАТОРСКАГО ВЕЛИЧЕСТВА рукою написано:

„НИКОЛАЙ".

Печатано въ С.-Петербургѣ, при Сенатѣ.   Ноября 3 дня 1895 года.

The Manifesto of Emperor Nicholas II on the occasion of the birth of his daughter, Grand Duchess Olga. 3 November 1895. State Archive of the Russian Federation

Valentin Serov (1865–1911).
The Anointing of Emperor
Nicholas II. 1897.
From the Coronation Book
of Nicholas II. The Peterhof
Museum Complex

*Emperor Nicholas II,
Empress Alexandra Feodorovna
and Grand Duchess Olga.
1896. State Archive of
the Russian Federation*

be a real lady. Be patient and polite, try to help sisters in every possible way."[4]

In a year and a half Olga received a younger sister. "It is the second bright and happy day in our family life," the Emperor recorded in his *Diary* on 29 May 1897 at Tsarskoye Selo. "At 10:40 a.m. the Lord blessed us with a daughter — Tatyana. Tatyana weighs 8 … pounds and is 54 centimetres. Our eldest daughter is very funny with her."[5] Grand Duke Konstantin Konstantinovich heard from the Tsar that his daughters Olga and Tatyana were named after the main female characters in Pushkin's novel *Eugene Onegin*[6]. The family was happy with its children. Nicholas wrote with a feeling of joy to his mother: "Our little daughters are growing and turning into delightful and merry girls… Olga speaks both Russian and English equally well. She adores her younger sister. Tatyana seems to us, understandably, a very beautiful child. She has

Grand Duchesses Olga and Tatyana. 1898. State Archive of the Russian Federation

[4] State Archive of the Russian Federation, fund 673, l. 1, No 71, fol. 7.

[5] State Archive of the Russian Federation, fund 601, l. 1., No 237.

[6] State Archive of the Russian Federation, fund 660, l. 1, No 50, fol. 67.

dark and large eyes. She is constantly in good humour and allows herself to cry only once a day, this happens, without fail, after her bath, when they feed her. The cossacks, soldiers and negroes are her best friends and she greets them all as she goes down the corridor."[7]

Almost two years passed after Tatyana's birth. The royal couple waited for a new addition to the family. The country needed a heir! But on 14 June 1899 at Peterhof, where the imperial family lived, a daughter was born again. They named her Marie. The parents were happy that a healthy child was born, but many members of the large royal family could not conceal their disappointment. Even the "dearest Grandmama", Queen Victoria, wrote on 2 (14 Old Style) July 1899 to Nicholas: "...I regret the 3rd girl for the country. I know that a Heir would be more welcome than a daughter."[8]

Two years later the country waited with sinking hearts for news about the birth of the fourth child to the Emperor's family. On 5 June 1901, at 6 o'clock in the morning, Anastasia was born at Peterhof. "Alix feels wonderful — but my Lord! What a disappointment!.. A fourth daughter!" exclaimed in her diary the Empress's sister, Grand Duchess Xenia Alexandrovna.[9] "My Lord, everybody felt disappointment instead of joy, because they waited a Heir," wrote Grand Duke Konstantin Konstantinovich[10].

In a month after the birth of the fourth daughter the imperial couple began to regularly meet a certain Mr. Philippe. He was a Frenchman from Lyons and had a reputation of hypnotist allegedly curing nervous disorders. In his homeland Philippe was prosecuted for medical practice without a diploma and was regarded a charlatan. However, he had the power to suggest to the Empress that if she would follow his advice she would certainly bear a son. In the summer of 1902 the thirty-year old Empress, mother of four children, influenced by Philippe's prophecies, concluded that she was pregnant. The news became generally known. All — and the Empress more than others — expected that the heir

[7] State Archive of the Russian Federation, fund 642, l. 1, No 2324, fol. 56–56v.

[8] State Archive of the Russian Federation, fund 601, l. 1, No 1194, fols. 95v–96.

[9] State Archive of the Russian Federation, fund 662, l. 1. No 16, fol. 135v.

[10] State Archive of the Russian Federation, fund 660, l. 1, No 48, fol. 86.

Emperor Nicholas II and Empress Alexandra Feodorovna.
1898. State Archive of the Russian Federation

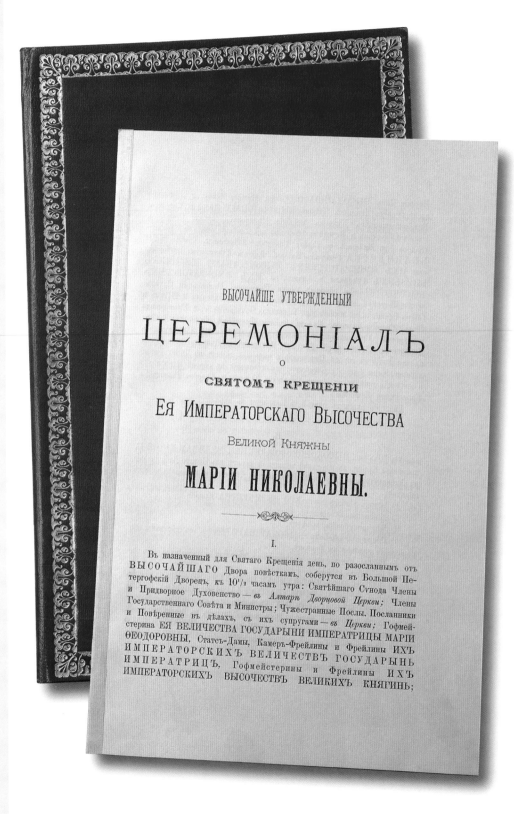

*The Procedure of Baptism
of Grand Duchess Marie
Nikolayevna. 1899.
State Archive of
the Russian Federation*

ВЫСОЧАЙШЕ УТВЕРЖДЕННЫЙ

ЦЕРЕМОНІАЛЪ

о

СВЯТОМЪ КРЕЩЕНІИ

Ея Императорскаго Высочества

Великой Княжны

МАРІИ НИКОЛАЕВНЫ.

I.

Въ назначенный для Святаго Крещенія день, по разосланнымъ отъ ВЫСОЧАЙШАГО Двора повѣсткамъ, соберутся въ Большой Петергофскій Дворецъ, къ 10¹/₂ часамъ утра: Святѣйшаго Сунода Члены и Придворное Духовенство — *въ Алтарь Дворцовой Церкви*; Члены Государственнаго Совѣта и Министры; Чужестранные Послы, Посланники и Повѣренные въ дѣлахъ, съ ихъ супругами — *въ Церкви*; Гофмейстерина ЕЯ ВЕЛИЧЕСТВА ГОСУДАРЫНИ ИМПЕРАТРИЦЫ МАРИИ ѲЕОДОРОВНЫ, Статсъ-Дамы, Камеръ-Фрейлины и Фрейлины ИХЪ ИМПЕРАТОРСКИХЪ ВЕЛИЧЕСТВЪ ГОСУДАРЫНЬ ИМПЕРАТРИЦЪ, Гофмейстерины и Фрейлины ИХЪ ИМПЕРАТОРСКИХЪ ВЫСОЧЕСТВЪ ВЕЛИКИХЪ КНЯГИНЬ;

*Grand Duchesses Olga, Tatyana and Marie. 1900.
State Archive of the Russian Federation*

Grand Duchesses Olga, Tatyana and Marie. Tsarskoye Selo. 1900. State Archive of the Russian Federation

Grand Duchesses Olga and Tatyana. Tsarskoye Selo. 1900. State Archive of the Russian Federation

Empress Alexandra Feodorovna and Grand
Duchess Anastasia. 1901. Below, the autograph
of Alexandra Feodorovna: Alix. 1901.
State Archive of the Russian Federation

Grand Duchess Olga.
Tsarskoye Selo. 1904.
State Archive of
the Russian Federation.
First publication

Grand Duchess Tatyana.
Tsarskoye Selo. 1904.
State Archive of the Russian
Federation. First publication

Grand Duchess Marie.
Tsarskoye Selo. 1904.
State Archive of
the Russian Federation

Grand Duchess Anastasia.
Tsarskoye Selo. 1904.
State Archive of
the Russian Federation

would be born, but the miracle did not happen. Grand Duke Konstantin Konstantinovich wrote in his diary about the events which took place at Peterhof in August 1902: "...from 8 August we have been waiting every day for confirmation of the Empress's pregnancy. Now we have suddenly learned that that she is not pregnant, indeed that there never was any pregnancy, and that the symptoms that led to suppose it were in fact only anaemia! What a disappointment for the Tsar and Tsarina! Poor things! Alix sent news of the sad discovery to Mama and my wife. Alix cried a lot when doctors Ott and Gunst, who were at last admitted to see her, determined that that not only was there no pregnancy, but there never had been."[11]

After the Empress's false pregnancy in 1902, Philippe prophesied that the Empress would have a son if she asked for the protection of St Serafim of Sarov. The saint was unknown in the Orthodox calendar, but it was discovered that there had been a monk of the name of Serafim whose life was a model of virtue and who had the repute of performing miracles. The Emperor demanded the Holy Synod to canonize Father Serafim. Pobedonostsev, the Procurator of the Holy Synod, tried to explain that a man could not be proclaimed a saint by imperial order. Alexandra Feodorovna is said to have answered: "The Emperor can do anything." Father Serafim was canonized in 1903. The royal family made a travel to Sarov for revering his relics in a hope for God's grace. The prayers of Alexandra Feodorovna were heard!

On 30 July 1904 the long-awaited heir was born at Peterhof. Nicholas II wrote in his *Diary*: "A great and unforgettable day for us, during which we were clearly visited by the grace of God. At 1:15 in the afternoon Alix gave birth to a son, whom we named Alexei as we prayed. Everything happened remarkably quickly — at least for me. In the morning I went to visit Mama as usual, after which I went to find Alix for lunch. She was already upstairs, and half an hour afterwards the happy event occurred. There are no

[11] State Archive of the Russian Federation, fund 660, l. 1, No 50, fol. 134.

Tsesarevich Alexis.
1904. State Archive of
the Russian Federation

words to thank God enough for sending us this comfort in a time of sore trials."[12]

According to the laws of the Russian Empire, before the birth of a son to the reigning Emperor, the title of the Heir belonged to his younger brother, the next in line. Nicholas had two brothers, George and Michael. George, who became the Heir to the throne at the moment of Nicholas's accession, died in 1899 from consumption after he had fallen from a bicycle. His title, according to the Manifesto of 28 June 1899, passed to the next brother, Grand Duke Michael Alexandrovich. The new manifesto, of 30 July 1904, declared: "From now on, in accordance with the fundamental laws of the Empire, the imperial title of the Heir Tsesarevich and all

[12] State Archive of the Russian Federation, fund 601, l. 1, No. 247, fols. 186–187.

23

[13] State Archive of the Russian Federation, fund 660, l. 1, No. 53, fol. 175.

The Diary of Nicholas II. 1904. The entry of 30 July 1904 about the birth of Tsesarevich Alexis. State Archive of the Russian Federation

the rights pertaining to it, belong to Our Son Alexis." Grand Duke Konstantin Konstantinovich wrote in his diary: " What a joy!. Russia has waited 10 years for an Heir, and now it has happened. Soon we heard the canons begin firing — a 301 gun salute."[13] The baby was very large — he weighed 11 pounds and measured 58 centimeters.

On 11 August the christening ceremony of the newly born Tsesarevich took place. The procession went to the Great Peterhof Palace. The festive gilded coach in which Alexis was brought, was accompanied by a convoy of the Cavalry Guards. Princess Marie Golitsyna, Mistress of the Robe, carried the boy to the church in her arms. To avoid slipping and not to drop the royal baby, the honourable lady had pieces of fabric pasted to the soles of her shoes. The god-parents of the Heir were the kings of England, Denmark, the German Kaiser William II, dukes and grand dukes. "What a very kind thought that was of yours to ask me to be Godfather to your little boy!

You can well imagine what out joy was when we read your telegram announcing his birth! 'Was lange währt, wird gut,' says an old German proverb, so may it be with this little dear one! May he grow to be a brave soldier and a wise and powerful statesman! And may God's blessing always rest on him and preserve him from all harm of body and soul. May he always be as a ray of sunshine to you both during your life, as he is now in the time of the trial!" wrote to Nicholas his "devoted and affectionate cousin Willy" — William II, who ten years later would begin a terrible bloody war against Russia, the war

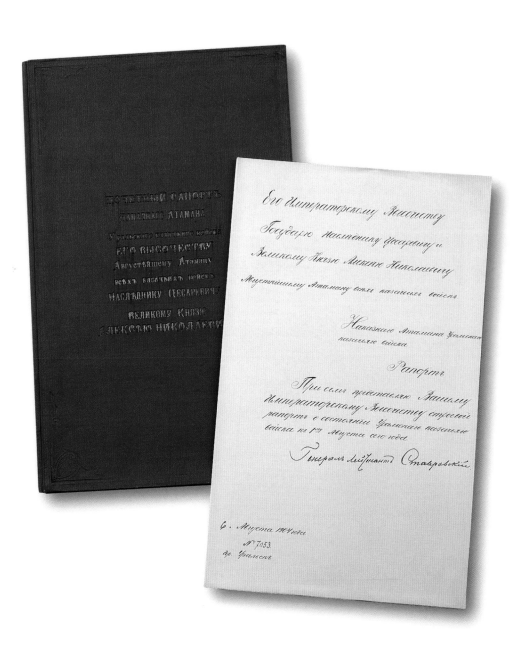

Honourary report of the Ataman of the Urals Cossack Army to Tsesarevich Alexis. 6 August 1904. State Archive of the Russian Federation

Tsesarevich Alexis with his mother Alexandra Feodorovna. [1906]. Tsarskoye Selo. State Archive of the Russian Federation

which eventually would become fatal not only for the Russian Emperor, but for the Kaiser himself.

During the christening ceremony Alexis was awarded the orders of St Andrew the First-Called, St Alexander Nevsky, the White Eagle, St Anne and St Stanislas; he was enrolled in the crew of the Guards and of the 89th Infantry White Sea Regiment, and appointed the Ataman of the Cossack Troops.

The choice of the name was a surprise for many people. Some caustic tongues remembered the son of Peter the Great. But the Emperor himself explained his decision: the heir was named in honour of his favourite Tsar Alexei Mikhailovich, nicknamed the "Mild", who reigned in the seventeenth century.

The little Alexis became the centre of the family's life. The Empress wrote from Peterhof to he husband who left for the Don to review the troops: "I am sure you miss Baby love; he is too sweet. Indeed one understands why God has just sent him this year to us and he has come as a real Sunbeam. God never forgets one, that is true. And now you have him to work for and to bring up to your ideas, so as that he can help you when he is a big boy. I assure you one sees him daily grow."[14]

All this bustle, however, did not trouble the little Tsarevich, who grew without knowing about the future awaiting him beyond the threshold of his nursery. But Fate seemed to mark Alexis by its fatal stamp from the first days of his life: the boy inherited, with the genes of the English royal house, a serious and then practically incurable illness — haemophilia. From this debilitating illness suffered Leopold, Queen Victoria's son, and several of her grandsons and great-grandsons. The illness took the life of Alexandra Feodorovna's brother and two nephews. The most characteristic clinical symptom of this disease was that the blood had not the power of coagulating which led to abundant, sometimes mortal bleedings. Bleedings into joints — haemarthrosis — were not infrequent. In Alexis's case, attacks of haemarthrosis were usually accompanied by strong pains, fever and prolonged lack

[14] State Archive of the Russian Federation, fund 601, l. 1, No. 1148, fol. 123v.

Tsesarevich Alexis on the yacht Standart. 1906.
State Archive of the Russian Federation

of force. Only males are affected by haemophilia, but the pathological gene is transmitted from generation to generation by the women to their male children. Probably, the gene mutation occurred with Queen Victoria, and the illness transmitted by her daughter through a generation, made unhappy not a single royal family in Europe.

In several months after the birth of Alexis his parents discovered the symptoms of his disease. Nicholas II wrote in his *Diary*: "8 September 1904… Alix and I were very worried because little Alexis started bleeding from the navel, and it continued on and off until the evening."[15] Grand Duchess Marie Pavlovna (the younger) wrote in her memoirs: "There is no doubt that the parents were quickly advised as to the nature of their son's illness. Nobody ever knew what emotions were aroused in them by this horrible certainty, but from that moment, troubled and apprehensive, the Empress's character underwent a change, and her health, physical as well as moral, altered."[16] "The healthy blood of the Romanovs could not win over the diseased blood of the Hesse-Darmstadt line, and the innocent child had to suffer from the negligence revealed by the Russian court in the choice of the bride for Nicholas II," wrote in his memoirs Voyeikov, the Commandant of the Palace.[17]

The lack of official information led to all sorts of conjectures. There were several reasons for such seemingly unexplainable secrecy. First, the parents believed that the child's disease is the family's misfortune that must not be known to outside people. Second, the information was concealed for the sake of state interests. The admission that the long-awaited heir to the throne suffers from a disease which has unpredictable consequences, could arise serious political problems. For the boy's mother, the thought that it was she who caused his sufferings, became a constant psychological trauma from which she could never recover. Each day of the struggle for Alexis's life took away her inner forces.

[15] *Dnevniki imperatora Nikolaya II*, Moscow, 1991, p. 228.

[16] Grand Duchess Marie of Russia, *Things I Remember*, London, 1930, p. 58.

[17] V. N. Voyeikov, *S tsariom I bez tsaria*, Helsingfors, 1933, pp. 182–183.

Tsesarevich Alexis. 1907. State Archive of the Russian Federation

Alexei had a particularly strong crisis at Spala, a lodge in Byelorussia, where the royal family went for hunting. Jumping out of a boat to the bank, the boy felt a sharp pain in his groin and hip. Doctors found a quickly growing haematoma or swelling. Nicholas described Alexis's state in his letter to his mother: "The days from 6 to 10 October were the most difficult. The poor child suffered greatly, pains tormented him by spasms which repeated almost every quarter of an hour. Owing to high temperature he was delirious day and night, he would sit in his bed, and the movement immediately caused pain. He almost could not sleep or even cry and only moaned and said: 'Lord, have mercy.' I could hardly stay in the room, but I had to replace Alix near him because she, understandably, got tired spending whole days at his bedside. She could bear this trial better than me when Alexis was bad, but now, when, thanks to God, the danger has gone away, she feels the consequence of what she suffered and it has affected her poor heart."[18]

Grigory Rasputin

It was precisely during the night of 10 October that Rasputin's telegram came which informed that the child would not die. Many witnesses described this scene, making different accents depending on their attitude to the Empress and Rasputin, but nobody even tried to get an insight into the hidden thoughts and feelings of the mother who saw a true miracle — the recovery of her son. In the future Alexandra Feodorovna, like a drug addict dependent on a drug, could not live without Rasputin's consolations. Two forces irrepressibly attracted the unfortunate mother to him: a fear to lose her child and a hope for his recovery. She perceived him as a true Russian *moujik* speaking in the name of entire Russia and knowing what to do — a real "God's man". And Rasputin, who perfectly understood his role in the life of

[18] State Archive of the Russian Federation, fund 642, l. 1, No 2332, fols. 20–21.

the royal family, constantly suggested to the Empress that "the Tsarevich will life as long as I am alive." These words also proved prophetic — the imperial family was shot only a year and a half after his death.

"All lucky families are similar, each unlucky family is unlucky in its own way," as Leo Tolstoy wrote at the beginning of his novel *Anna Karenina*. The same words might be made an epigraph to a narrative about the family of the last reigning

Tsesarevich Alexis.
Tsarskoye Selo. 1907

[19] *Dnevniki imperatora Nikolaya II,* Moscow, 1991, p. 354.

Romanov. The parents' happiness was in their children and their pain was the incurable illness of their only son. But this pain drew them all together and turned the narrow world of the family into a circle of like-minded persons.

"Nicholas II felt himself best of all in the bosom of his family. He adored his wife and children. He was on friendly terms with his children; he took part in their games, readily went to promenade with them and they paid him with passionate and genuine love. He liked to read aloud Russian classics of literature to his family. In general, it is even difficult to imagine a more ideal, homely atmosphere than that reigning in the royal family. Against the background of the general dissolution of family morals, both in Russian and Western European society, the family of the Russian Sovereign was no less rare than sparkling phenomenon," this is how the imperial family was characterized by General Mosolov, Head of the Chancellery of the Imperial Court, in his memoirs.[19]

Emperor Nicholas II with his family.
St Petersburg. 1904

Empress Alexandra Feodorovna and her daughters. The Lower Dacha, Alexandria

*"Lovely Alexandria", "dear Peterhof",
"our charming home" – such definitions can
be often met in the Diaries of Nicholas II,
and such an attitude to the cosy seaside
palace would remain many years later.*

*Nicholas II and his family.
Peterhof. 1906*

During the reign of Nicholas II, Peterhof remained the official summer residence of the imperial family which used to spend there two to three summer months every year, from 1895 to 1914, sometimes staying there until late autumn.

Their permanent and favourite place was the Alexandria Park, a private possession of the imperial family. In this large, remote park spreading along the seashore, the predecessors of Nicholas II built a number of small country palaces and cottages, a home church known as the Chapel, and all sorts of auxiliary buildings.

Dowager Empress Marie Feodorovna, Nicholas II's mother, lived in the Cottage Palace, while the Farm Palace was often visited by the family's closest relatives – the Tsar's sister Xenia Alexandrovna with her husband, Grand Duke Alexander Mikhailovich, Elizabeth Feodorovna (Ella), the sister of Empress Alexandra Feodorovna, and others. The so-called Lower Dacha or the Lower Palace was built specially for Nicholas II on the seashore in the north-eastern part of the park. The remote position of Alexandria from noisy Peterhof and the complete absence of undesirable people in this carefully guarded private residence which was completely isolated from the very beginning, created an illusion of freedom, calm and thoughtless existence.

It was there, at the Lower Dacha, that Nicholas II and Alexandra Feodorovna spent the first summer of their family life in 1895.

Nicholas II wrote in his diary on 27 May 1895: "...We've arrived in Peterhof at 4 o'clock. I came to our lovely Alexandria with a feeling of joy and sadness and entered our house by the sea. It seems so strange to live here with my wife. Although there is not enough space here, the rooms are pretty and the premises are ideal. The new room below, by the dining room (for Alix) is wonderfully decorated. But the main thing, the beauty of the entire home, is the proximity of the sea!"[1]

The Lower Dacha was a two-storeyed building. Originally, on the site of the dismantled signal telegraph (designed by Joseph Charlemagne in 1833), a small pavilion with a tall slender tower imitating Italian architecture was erected, on the orders of Alexander III, for the heir apparent in 1883–85. Its design was approved on 26 May 1882. The author of the project was the then young architect, Adjunct-Professor Anthony Tomishko (1851–1900). As the architect himself noted, "the building of the New Palace is designed in keeping with the style of a villa (country residence) of the Italian Renaissance, on the orders of His Majesty."[2]

The new palace was a small four-storeyed building with asymmetrically placed balconies, terraces and loggias. Next to the main block stood a six-storeyed building with a belvedere crowned with a spire. The tower had a good look from the seaside and was a prominent vertical feature of the park. In architectural terms, the northern façade was particularly impressive. The two-flight staircase, fenced by an elegant metal

Design for the reconstruction of the Lower Dacha (a version). By Anthony Tomishko. Late 1890s. Watercolour. View from the park. In the foreground, the children's apartments. The Peterhof Museum Complex. First publication

The Lower Dacha of Nicholas II. Alexandria. View from the Gulf of Finland. On the tower, a flag with the coat-of-arms of Alexandria. Photograph of 1905–15. The Peterhof Museum Complex. First publication

railing, led from the park directly to the first floor, into the loggia over which was a spacious terrace. Using all sorts of building materials and revealing their decorative properties — texture and colour — the architect gave a more up-to-date look to the traditional type of park pavilion with a belvedere.

The basement of the building and key blocks were made of pink-red granite; the ground floor was faced with grey Putilovo slabs; the walls were of high-quality yellow and terra-cotta decorative bricks alternating as horizontal strips of diverse width. Many architectural details — the columns, pilasters, window surrounds, arches, cornices and balustrades — were made of light grey sandstone. The layout of the living interiors was also altered in keeping with a novel trend. The previously popular suite design almost disappeared. Now the rooms were grouped around the central hall which could be passed through, while others were isolated one from another.

The ground floor was used for all kinds of services. In the vestibule adorned with artificial marble, a man in eighteenth-century costume was usually on duty, who accompanied ministers and other visitors who were given attendance, to the study of the Emperor. The main staircase enlivened by decorative paintings and mirrors, led to the first floor where the studies of Nicholas II and Alexandra Feodorovna, the Dining Room and the Pink Drawing Room (the only passage room)

were located. Private apartments occupied the second floor: the Bedrooms, Dressing Room and Bathroom, and Small Drawing Room (Coffee Room). The interiors of the third floor, known as "ship apartments", were a sort of Nicholas II's study.

The Study of the Emperor was particularly notable among the interiors of the palace. Its walls were largely covered with carved panels of dark walnut. The furniture matched the decor of the walls: sofas, cabinets and shelves were built into the panelling — a device characteristic of the Art Nouveau style in general and of the Lower Dacha in particular. The study had two desks: one of them was used by Nicholas II when he listened to reports and the other was employed as a writing table for work. All the furniture was upholstered in black morocco, and the leather chairs and armchairs were adorned with stamped designs. Above the panelling, the walls were lined with blue silk; on the windows hung brocade curtains covered with woven medallions of golden thread. Portraits of Peter the Great, Nicholas I and Alexander III, the father of the Tsar, hung on the walls. (The portrait of Alexander III was a work by Valentin Serov, who demonstrated his new painting at the Lower Dacha on 18 August 1899.)

Among other works of fine art decorating the walls were numerous watercolours by Sergei Solomko, Alexander Beggrow, Albert Benois, Mikhail Klodt, Michaly Zichy and

*Design for the reconstruction
of the Lower Dacha (a version).
By Anthony Tomishko.
1897. Watercolour.
View from the seaside.
In the foreground, a part
of the building constructed
by Tomishko in 1885.
The Peterhof Museum Complex.
First publication*

The Study of Emperor Nicholas II. The Lower Dacha,
Alexandria. On the table and walls are
photographs of members of the imperial family.
1927–32. The Peterhof Museum Complex.
First publication

Arseny Meshchersky representing landscapes and battle scenes. Additional decorative features were porcelain and silver dishes, vases and ewers of coloured glass.

In this study Nicholas II listened to several reports of his ministers and generals every day. Receptions of various delegations and commissions, sessions of the State Council took place in the Farm Palace, while official ceremonies were held in the Great Palace. Many outstanding state figures, such as Sergei Witte, Piotr Stolypin and Konstantin Pobedonostsev, visited the Lower Palace.

After morning coffee the Emperor used to go out for a walk and to visit his mother, Dowager Empress Marie Feodorovna. At one o'clock the family had a lunch to which some of relatives and an officer on duty were invited. Then followed another promenade, on horseback or in a carriage together with Alexandra Feodorovna, sea bathing, kayak boating, travels in a motor-boat, riding a bicycle in a park and playing tennis. At five o'clock tea was served. Then Nicholas read telegrams and newspapers, returned to his study and continued to receive

**Ernest Liphart (1847–1932). Emperor Nicholas II
in the Uniform of the Aide-de-Camp of the Mounted
Regiment of the Life Guards with the Star
of the Order of St Andrew the First-Called and Badges
of Russian and Foreign Orders. Before 1913.
The Peterhof Museum Complex**

visitors. At eight o'clock a family dinner was held at which some of the relatives were also usually present. After dinner the Emperor worked in his study or relaxed together with his family.

The first interior in which visitors found themselves after the Main Staircase, was the Pink Drawing Room of Alexandra Feodorovna. The interior was decorated in the Art Nouveau style by Feodor Meltzer, who owned a furniture factory, in the early 1900s. The walls of the drawing room were decorated with wainscotting. Over the panels, painted in white enamel in imitation of ebony, was striped wallpaper with a minute flower pattern of roses. The white lacquered soft furniture was upholstered in cretonne with large red roses and green leaves scattered all over. The rose motif or its colour were employed everywhere: roses were carved on the furniture; pink cloth covered one of the tables, and another was lined with a cloth featuring a wreath of bright red roses under glass. The furniture had simple rectangular shapes or slightly curving outlines. The corner sofa built into a recess made up a single whole with the wall. The contour of the recess was echoed by the two-tiered, three-leaved mirror fixed on a shelf at the back of a sofa, on which were displayed crystal vases of Russian and Venetian work, Danish and Russian porcelain of the late nineteenth and early twentieth centuries characteristic of the Art Nouveau style. The bronze lamp with a rod styled as a water lily with whimsically bent stems, exquisite shapes of leaves and buds of flowers, attracted one's particular attention.

Among paintings and watercolours by Nikolai Samokish, Sergei Solomko, Albert Benois, Yelena Samokish-Sudkovskaya, basically battle scenes, a portrait of Alexandra Feodorovna painted by the amateur artist Captain Shipov, as well as the three photographic portraits of the Heir Tsarevich Alexis, were noteworthy. The decor of the Reception Room was enhanced by a carpet of soft pistachio colour with a checked pattern.

The principle of unity was used even more consistently in the design of the Dining Room. The walls of this room were decorated with high panels painted in white enamel and with shelves over them. Mounted in the panels were folding shelves, a two-tiered buffet with mirrors and sliding doors in the centre concealing a lifting machine. The mantelpiece with mirrors and shelves was also faced with white wood. In the centre of

The Reception Room of Alexandra Feodorovna. The Lower Palace. Alexandria. To the left, on the wall hangs a portrait of Alexandra Feodorovna in a kokoshnik and Russian dress produced by Captain P. Shipov in 1902. 1927–32. The Peterhof Museum Complex. First publication

Upholstery fabric (rep). England. Early 20th century From the Drawing Room of Alexandra Feodorovna. The Lower Palace, Alexandria. The Peterhof Museum Complex

Ilya Galkin (1860–1915). Empress Alexandra Feodorovna in a State Court Costume with the Star and Ribbon of the Order of St Catherine and Badges of Other Orders. 1895. The Peterhof Museum Complex

*Mikhail Rundaltsev (1871–1935).
Portrait of Empress
Alexandra Feodorovna.
1905. Etching. Hermitage,
St Petersburg*

**Bookplate
of Alexandra
Feodorovna.
The Peterhof
Museum Complex**

*Dress of Empress Alexandra Feodorovna. Russia.
1900s–1910s. Silk, chiffon, lace and embroidery.
The Peterhof Museum Complex*

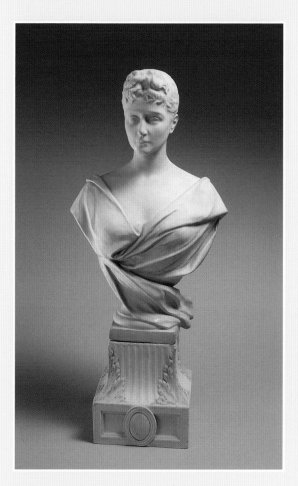

*Bust of Empress Alexandra Feodorovna.
Modelled by Mark Antokolsky (1843–1902).
Pottery workshop of Théodore Deck, Paris.
1896–1900. Earthenware, coloured glazing.
The Peterhof Museum Complex*

*Band with the monogram of Empress
Alexandra Feodorovna. Russia. 1910.
Painted moire. The Peterhof Museum
Complex. First publication*

*Cup and saucer with the monogram of Empress
Alexandra Feodorovna under the crown.
The Imperial Porcelain Factory. St Petersburg.
1902 (saucer), 1914 (cup). Porcelain, painted in cobalt
blue under a glaze and in colours over a glaze and
gilded. The Peterhof Museum Complex*

The Dining Room. The Lower Dacha, Alexandria. 1927–32. The Peterhof Museum Complex

the room stood an expanding dinner table and a buffet table with folding shelves. The furnishings were marked by slightly rounded forms.

The tables and chairs were also upholstered in light and dark blue leather; the floor was covered with a plush greenish-blue carpet with deep blue medallions; on the windows were straw-coloured curtains with dark pale poppies and green leaves. Displayed on the fireplace, in the recess and on the shelves were porcelain articles of Russian work in the Art Nouveau style, coloured and transparent glass and crystal vases and bowls. As a whole the decor of the Dining Room was reminiscent of a suite in the royal yacht called "Standart".

"Built in Denmark, it was considered one of the best vessels of this kind in the world. With its 45000 ton displacement, the yacht was painted black, with gilded decorations on the prow and stern. The 'Standart' had high nautical qualities and was provided with a great comfort."[3] Usually every year for no less than two weeks the family sailed to the sea on the 'Standart' travelling around skerries or along the gulf. "We moved with quiet joy to our 'Standart' which glittered and glowed in the sun."[4]

Rowing, picnics on islands, small dancing parties with local people on the shores, bathing, games and listening to balalaika concerts and other amusements were captured on numerous amateur photographs taken by Nicholas II himself or by other members of the family. The representation of the "Standard" by N. D. Prokofyev, numerous photographs of the yacht, as well as seascapes by Mikhail Tkachenko, Iosif Krachkovsky and Albert Benois decorated the walls of the room.

The room also housed two sketches by Ilya Repin for his paintings "The Marriage of Nicholas II and Alice of Hesse" and "The Zaporozhye Cossacks Writing a Mocking Letter to the Turkish Sultan".

On the personal order of Nicholas II, Meltzer partly altered the decor of the Study of Alexandra Feodorovna – new furniture of Karelian birch was manufactured. The same wood was used for details of architectural decor: the window surrounds, cornices, plinths and baguettes; even the fireplace was faced with it. The shelves, caskets and a clock case were also made of Karelian birch.

The furniture produced to designs by Meltzer was decorated with gilded bronze mounts and, like the walls, was upholstered in cretonne with finely spaced stylized bunches of cornflowers woven with bands and installed to divide the room in two parts: the Study as such with a fireplace and a desk in the corner and the Boudoir with a sofa, a coach and soft armchairs. The floor of the room was covered with a velvet carpet remarkable for its overall design of large light grey flowers with rocaille scrolls. A notable feature of the interior were porcelain articles: bowl-shaped table lamps, Danish vases and Venetian glass items from Murano. The walls were decorated with paintings and portraits by Nikolai Ulyanov, Sergei Solomko, watercolours of marines and landscapes by Yelizaveta Bem, Alexander Beggrow and other artists.

The third floor served as a Bedroom. Its walls were faced, above a low panelling, with white cretonne having a design of blue cornflowers. At the top, the walls were adorned with a moulded profile cornice and a painted frieze, similarly to the previously designed interiors of the palace. The ceiling was adorned with a moulded plant design. The floor was covered with a lilac plush carpet featuring bright grey wreaths or medallions all over it. The Bedroom was provided with mahogany furniture upholstered in cretonne. In the centre stood a double bed separated by a screen. On the walls were numerous icons, decorative bands, Easter eggs and phototypes from paintings of Biblical themes by English and German masters. There was a small library in the Bedroom which reflected spiritual interests of Nicholas II and Alexandra

Dish. The Imperial Porcelain Factory. St Petersburg. 1881–94. Porcelain, painted in colours over a glaze. The Lower Dacha, Alexandria. The Peterhof Museum Complex

Vase. The Imperial Porcelain Factory, St Petersburg. 1906. Porcelain, painted in colours under a glaze. The Lower Dacha, Alexandria. The Peterhof Museum Complex. First publication

Feodorovna. Among the books in the library were the lives of saints, such as St Sergius of Radonezh, St Anna of Kashin, St Serafim of Sarov, etc. Next to the Bedroom was the Dressing Room, decorated in the manner matching that of the Bedroom and the Bathroom and similar in its size and decor to a cabin on a ship. The walls in these rooms were also amply decorated with photographs of family members.

From the Bedroom, through the Room of the Lady-in-Waiting, one could pass to a small drawing room, generally known as the Coffee Room, where the entire family liked to gather in the evening. Here Nicholas II read aloud "A History of the Life-Guards" and pasted photographs into an album. Photography was very popular with the family and there were more than 1000 photographs which vividly recorded various events and peculiar features of daily life of the imperial family.

The trimming of the Coffee Room was reminiscent of the Bedroom: low mahogany panels, cretonne with garlands of flowers on the walls, a coffered and moulded ceiling. The furniture characteristic of the Art Nouveau style — small tables, armchairs on thin, exquisitely bowed legs and built-in corner sofas with shelves — were supplied by the same Meltzer. The rooms at the tower and terraces were provided with then very fashionable bent furniture of the Thonet Company.

All alterations in the decor were connected with the building of a new wing on the southern side of the palace. Its project was designed by Anthony Tomishko in 1895 and the work was carried out in 1896–97. The new wing, named "the children's apartments", was linked by a gallery with the old part of the building. Using the same devices of the artistic decoration of

*The Alexandrine Service.
The Imperial Porcelain
Factory, St Petersburg.
1899–1903. Porcelain
painted in colours
over a glaze and gilded.
Belonged to Empress
Alexandra Feodorovna.
The Peterhof Museum
Complex*

*The Purple Service. The Imperial Porcelain Factory,
St Petersburg. 1904–08. Porcelain painted in colours
over a glaze and gilded. Belonged to the imperial
family. The Peterhof Museum Complex*

*Goblets. The Imperial Glass Works, St Petersburg.
1899–1903. Colourless glass and coloured enamels.
From the Reception Room of the Cottage Palace.
The Peterhof Museum Complex*

Easter eggs with the monograms of Emperor Nicholas II
and Empress Alexandra Feodorovna under the crown.
The Imperial Porcelain Factory, St Petersburg.
1896–1900s. Glazed and gilded porcelain.
The Peterhof Museum Complex

Swan. Modelled by T. C. Madsen (1880–1965).
The Royal Porcelain Factory, Copenhagen. After 1906.
Porcelain, painted in colours under a glaze.
The Lower Dacha, Alexandria. The Peterhof Museum Complex

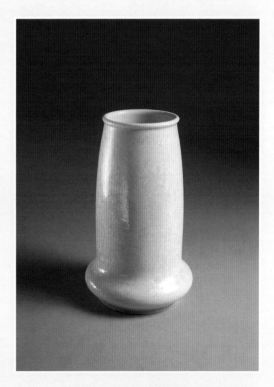

Vase with "yellow crystals". The Imperial
Porcelain Factory, St Petersburg. 1906.
Porcelain, crystal glazing.
The Peterhof Museum Complex.
First publication

Yegor Meyer (1820–1867).
View of the Church of the
Great Peterhof Palace.
1842. Watercolour.
The Peterhof Museum Complex

The room of Grand Duchess Tatyana. The Lower Dacha, Alexandria. On the pillow are the embroidered letter "T" under the crown and the date "1914". 1927. The Peterhof Museum Complex. First publication

façades and the same building materials, the architect attained an impression of the organic compositional unity of both, functionally independent parts of the building. The interior decor and furnishing of the rooms were also made by Meltzer and served as an example for the reconstruction of an old room in the palace. Meltzer was again invited in the 1900s, when draperies and upholstery of the walls and the furniture were replaced in many of the rooms as were other elements of the interior decor.

The necessity to extend the palace was due to the growth of the imperial family. Starting from 1895, with intervals of about two years, Alexandra Feodorovna gave birth to four daughters. The eldest of them, Olga, was born on 3 November 1895 at Tsarskoye Selo. The other children, however, were born at Peterhof.

The family spent the summer months of 1896 and 1897 at the Farm Palace. "We settled at the Farm for this summer, because a second house is being added by the sea," Nicholas II wrote.[5] On 29 May 1897 at 10:40 a.m. the second daughter was born and named Tatyana. 101 guns sounded in salute from the military harbour and the Peter and Paul Fortress; the mass was served at the Alexandria Church and the next day at St Isaac's Cathedral in St Petersburg, where a manifesto devoted to this event was then read. Bulletins about the health of the Empress and the Grand Duchess were issued every day. The baptism of Tatyana took place on Sunday, 8 June 1897. Special trains were arranged from St Petersburg and Krasnoye Selo and special rooms were allotted both in the Great Palace and in the house of the Minister of the Imperial Court for those who possessed the right to come to the court. The ceremony of baptism was worked out in detail. By 10:30 a.m. members of the Synod and priesthood gathered in the chancel; the State Council, ministers and diplomats, court ladies and gentlemen gathered in the tent by the Armorial Block, generals in the room in front of the Guards Room and the military in the Peter Hall, Room for the Lady-in-Waiting, White Hall and Chinese Room, top civil officials at the Secretary's Room and ladies from the city in the Blue Drawing Room and the Room for Cavaliers-in-Attendance. Ladies were to wear Russian-style costumes and gentlemen to be clad in full-dress uniform. The imperial family gathered in the inner apartments of the Armorial Block. The Grand Duchess was brought from the Farm Palace to the entrance of the Armorial Block in a festive gilded carriage harnessed with six horses, in the hands of the Mistress of the Court, Princess Golitsyna accompanied by the convoy and courtiers. Then she was brought in a basket to the Bedroom of the Armorial Block. The ceremonial procession from the Crimson Room of the Armorial Block proceeded through all its halls and rooms to the Church where Protopresbyter Ioann Yanyshev performed the rite of baptism. The grand princess was bestowed the Order of St Catherine with which all newly born grand duchesses were awarded.

The god-parents of Tatyana Nikolayevna were Marie Feodorovna and Grigory Alexandrovich, Nicholas II's brother, and numerous relatives of the royal and ducal dynasties of Europe. In the evening St Petersburg and Peterhof were fully illuminated. After the rite of baptism was performed, 101 shots of guns were made at the military landing-stage accompanied by the chime of all Peterhof churches. The Grand Duchess was brought through the Divan and Crown Rooms to the Oak Study and then, from the Sampsonius Entrance, was carried back to the Farm Palace. At the same day a reception of diplomats and a luncheon took place in the Peter and Merchant Halls and in the tent below, in the Armorial Block. The luncheon was held to the accompaniment of music.

Similar ceremonies with minor alterations were held to celebrate the birth and baptism of the next daughters. Marie was born on 14 June 1899 in the Lower Palace and baptized on 27 June 1899 in the Church of the Great Palace; Anastasia was born on 5 June 1901 at the Lower Dacha too and christened on 17 June 1901 in the same church. Somewhat later, on 30 June 1901, a church was laid out beyond the railway station at Peterhof, and consecrated, on 5 June 1903, to the holy martyr St Anastasia. In the Lower Palace the rooms of the daughters were located on the second and third floors of the new block. They were quite modest and similar in design: the traditional cretonne upholstery of the walls, oak parquet floors with walnut insets, window-sills and doors with amaranth friezes and mahogany panel along the bottom. The main attention was paid to the demands of hygiene and daily comfort. The interiors, however, had a merry and attractive appearance. They were given variety by the upholstery of the walls and furniture with a characteristic Art Nouveau design in which stylized motifs of flora and fauna were used. Depicted on the light

Eduard Hau (1807–1887). The Church of SS Peter and Paul in the Great Peterhof Palace. Watercolour. The Peterhof Museum Complex

Corner sofa with a high back.
The F. Meltzer Furniture
Factory, St Petersburg.
Late 19th century.
Walnut, bone, mirror,
velvet, inlay.
From the Drawing Room
of the grand duchesses.
The Lower Dacha,
Alexandria.
The Hermitage,
St Petersburg

Armchair. Early 20th century.
Mahogany, velvet. From the Drawing Room
of the grand duchesses. The Lower Dacha,
Alexandria. The Hermitage, St Petersburg

The Drawing Room
of the grand
duchesses.
The Lower Dacha,
Alexandria. 1932.
The Peterhof
Museum Complex

Empress Alexandra Feodorovna.
Photograph in a frame made at
Burmingham, England. 1900–10.
Silver, guilloche ornament
The Peterhof Museum Complex.
First publication

Nicholas II with his family. The Drawing Room of the grand
duchesses. The Lower Dacha, Alexandria. 1900s

Armchair. Early 20th century.
Mahogany, velvet. From the Drawing Room
of the grand duchesses. The Lower Dacha,
Alexandria. The Hermitage, St Petersburg

Armchair. The F. Meltzer Furniture Factory,
St Petersburg. Late 19th century.
Mahogany, velvet. From the Drawing Room
of the grand duchesses. The Lower Dacha,
Alexandria. The Hermitage, St Petersburg

OTMA. 1906. The Peterhof Museum Complex

*Grand Duchesses Olga and Tatyana
in the uniforms of the regiments
under their patronage.
Tsarskoye Selo [1913]. State Archive
of the Russian Federation*

*The patron's uniform of the 8th Uhlan
Resurrection Regiment of Her Imperial
Highness Tatyana Nikolayevna. 1910s.
The Tsarskoye Selo Museum Complex*

Uhlan officer's fur cap
(for the uniform).
The P. A. Fokin Military
Supply Factory,
St Petersburg. 1910s.
Cloth, leather and metal.
On the cockade, the
decoration "For Telish".
Belonged to Tsesarevich
Alexis. Museum of Artillery,
Engineering and Signal
Corps, St Petersburg

Grand Duchess Marie in the uniform
of the regiment under her patronage.
Tsarskoye Selo. [1913]. State Archive
of the Russian Federation

grey, cream or white background were large white lilies, red-pink poppies and blue cornflowers. The room was furnished with simple and austere furniture almost devoid of any decor, yet marked by lightness and elegance. Of particular interest was the furniture in Olga's room: it was painted green and upholstered in varicoloured velvet — large yellow flowers with long leaves on a grey ground, with peacocks spreading their tails. The armchairs and chairs were with high backs and wavelike bars, length- and cross-wise, thin legs and arm-rests. The furniture of similar refined shapes was in the daughters' drawing room. It was lined with velvet, varying in pattern and colour on all items: grey with pink and blue flowers, red and grey with the same pattern, brick-red plush with yellow flowers, grey with yellow flowers and with peacocks.

Such a diverse gamut instilled a life-asserting optimistic mood. The corner sofa with a mirror in this room was the favourite place for making photographs of the entire family. The decor of these children's rooms included articles of porcelain and glass: decorative vases and bowls, dishes, numerous figurines of animals by Russian and Dutch masters of the late nineteenth and early twentieth centuries; the walls were decorated with paintings and watercolours by popular artists of the period, but most often with icons and photographs.

Of particular interest among the interiors of the children's apartments were the rooms of Tsesarevich Alexis. The happy life of the Emperor's family was darkened by the lack of a heir to the throne. But at last, on 30 June 1904, the long-awaited event took place. On 11 August 1904 the baptism of the newly born heir took place in the SS Peter and Paul Church of the Great Palace. "The memorable day of the baptism of our beloved son. The morning was bright and warm. Until 9:30 golden carriages stood in front of the seaside house and three platoons, of the Convoy, Hussars and Ataman Troops. At five minutes to ten the procession began to move... The baptism began at 11 o'clock. Later I learned that the little Alexis was calm... The main god-parents were Mummy and Alexis."[6]

This ceremony was unusually solemn and luxurious. The festive carriage was harnessed with six horses and the train of attendants was also very impressive. The Order of St Andrew the First-Called was brought to the church on a golden dish. Numerous relatives of high rank came to the ceremony of baptism; even the elderly 87-year-old Christian IX, Alexis's grand-grandfather, arrived. Totally there were 1091 invited dignitaries, including forty members of the imperial family.

301 cannon shots were made, and church bells were ringing. The festive luncheon for 396 persons took place in the Great Palace. In the evening both capitals and Peterhof sparkled with illumination.

The joy of the family was immeasurable, but it turned out soon that the only son and heir is incurably ill with haemophilia and his life was in danger every moment. This factor made an indelible imprint on all aspects of the royal family's life and deprived it of peace and confidence for ever.

Alexis, a smart, charming and clever boy, was vivid and alert, but he suffered much already in his early years.

He was given separate apartments on the first floor. The main staircase with marble steps and massive handrails led from the vestibule upstairs. The vestibule and the staircase were decorated with twenty porcelain stands for flowers, vases and baskets. The abundance of flowers created a joyful, bright mood. Alexis's rooms were vast, with high ceilings, large windows, light and sunny. The apartments included the Reception Room and Bedroom of Alexis, the room of the sailor Derevenko put to guard the heir to the trone from accidental injures, the daytime nursery, buffet, bathroom, toilet room and a huge covered balcony.

Soon after Alexis's birth these rooms were renovated and furnished anew by Feodor Meltzer with furniture of white and bright maple and of white maple painted in imitation of lacquer and upholstered in cretonne of light shades with representations of lilies, poppies and carnations woven with bands. A piano of the Becker Company stood in the Reception Room, while in the Bedroom and Nursery, next to usual furniture, were children's washing table, stool, chairs and even a table for swaddling which were upholstered in white chamois; the walls were decorated with numerous photographs, engravings and watercolours with traditional subjects: parades, manoeuvres and the yacht "Standart". The decor here was added by porcelain statuettes and crystal vases.

The Nursery served for playing games and studies.

Lots of toys were presented to Alexis to distract him from lively games dangerous for his health. The room contained many toy porcelain and wooden figurines of animals and birds, whole armies of tin soldiers, puppet houses with furniture, all kinds of utensils, models of ships, a submarine, a fire-pump with barrels, a sledge harnessed with three toy horses, a dirigeable, a railway line, a box with a sabre, darts and wooden rifle, a toy fortress, a set of mosaics, a device for plaster casting, a stereoscope, albums for photographs and picture tinting, tennis rackets, balls and many other things. Alexis liked to play out of doors and to engage in physical labour when he felt himself well. In Alexandria, there was a field sown with rye where he could reap.

But owing to his illness the Tsesarevich was devoid of many activities and pastimes typical of his age. The successor's illness changed much in the mode of life of the royal family, the character of its relations with courtiers and even with members of the imperial family. Only doctors, teachers and the closest relatives knew about the boy's poor health. The family's world became even more closed and isolated. It is not a surprise that Grigory Rasputin, the only man who was able to exorcize Alexis's pain and to stop bleeding, acquired an exclusive influence upon the royal family and Alexandra Feodorovna in particular. Their acquaintance with Rasputin took place at Sergiyevka on 1 November 1905, on the estate of Anastasia Nikolayevna, the daughter of the King of Montenegro, then the wife of George Leuchtenbergsky-Romanovsky (in 1907 she married for the second time, Grand Duke Nikolai Nikolayevich the Younger). The further meetings with Rasputin took place also at Znamenka, the estate of Militsa Nikolayevna, Anastasia Nikolayevna's sister, the wife of Grand Duke Piotr Nikolayevich.

Tsesarevich Alexis. Photograph in a two-side frame. By Hjalmar Armfeldt. The Fabergé Company, St Petersburg. 1907–08. Silver guilt, enamel, guilloche ornament. On the one side Alexis is shown wearing *a sailor's jacket and a wide-brimmed hat, on the other in the uniform of the sailor of the yacht Standart. From the Study of Dowager Empress Marie Feodorovna. The Cottage Palace, the Peterhof Museum Complex*

Grigory Rasputin came to the Lower Dacha for the first time on 13 October 1906. The Tsar recorded: "At 6 o'clock Grigory came to us; he brought an icon of St Simeon of Verkhotursky, he saw our children and talked to them until 7:30."

Despite a constant threat to his life, however, Alexis was being prepared for the role of monarch from his childhood. He took part in receptions, parades and inspections. On 17 June 1907, during a celebration in honour of the Semionovsky Regiment which distinguished itself during the suppression of disturbances in Moscow, Nikolai II carried the Tsesarevich in his arms before the marching soldiers. "At 3 o'clock the entire Semionovsky Regiment has come to Alexandria. On greeting all the companies, we marched to music, at the head of the regiment, past our house to the glade where tables with tea and buns were laid."[8]

On 31 May 1907 the Tsar recorded in the Diary: "On the day of the regiment's festival Orlov brought a small size uniform of the uhlan regiment for Alexis."[9]

Children took part, together with their parents, in festivities dedicated to the 200th anniversary of the Battle of Poltava and the foundation of Peterhof which took place on 29 June 1909, the feast day of SS Peter and Paul. The children were present at the wedding ceremony of Nicholas II's brother-in-law Ioann

Konstantinovich with the Serbian Princess Yelena Petrovna on 21 August 1911. "On that day the seven-year successor Alexis wore the officer's uniform of the Imperial Household Riflemen. The youngest Grand Duchesses, who also for the first time put on Russian court dresses — white with pink flowers, but without trains, and pink kokoshniks, were charming."[10]

In August 1912 the entire family was present at the celebration devoted to the centenary of the Battle of Borodino in Moscow.

The eldest daughters, Olga and Tatyana, even took part in a military parade on 5 August 1913. At the head of the 8th Uhlan Voznesensky and the 3rd Hussar Elizavetgradsky Regiments, they marched, in a mounted line, before Nicholas II and Alexis and the younger sisters. Then all of them went to Alexandria, to the Lower Dacha. Many memorable events in the history of Russia are connected with the Lower Palace, beginning with visits of major political figures and ending with historic cataclysms. Thus, for example, in June 1897 the German Emperor William II arrived in Peterhof; in August 1897, Félix Faure, the President of the French Republic, visited the suburban residence; in June 1897, the Siamese Prince; and in July 1900, the Shah of Persia visited Peterhof. The guests attended not only official receptions and festive performances and illuminations, but visited Alexandria too. At the Lower Dacha Nicholas II signed the Manifest of 17 October which gave civic freedoms and summoned the State Duma or the Russian Parliament. The session of the First State Duma opened on 9 July 1906, the Second State Duma started on 3 June 1907. Decrees about them were signed at the Lower Palace. It was also here that Nicholas II received the news about the beginning of World War I, soon after Raymond Poincaré, the president of France, departed from Russia. The four-day visit of the French squadron headed by the French president was the last large-scale reception at Peterhof. It also included a visit to the Lower Dacha.

On 9 July 1914, as Nicholas II recorded, "at 11:30 Poincaré brought presents for Alix and our children."[11] The president himself handed the Légion d'Honneur to Alexis. On 3 August 1914 the imperial family left Peterhof for ever. "The weather was cool, in the daytime the sun peeped out from the clouds for several hours. We were at the mass and had a lunch in the rooms of the Farm Palace. I packed things and papers. I had a promenade with the daughters and we met Mummy near

Upholstery fabric (cretonne). England. Early 20th century. From the Reception Room of Tsarevich Alexis. The Lower Dacha, Alexandria. The Peterhof Museum Complex

The Reception Room of Tsesarevich Alexis. The Lower Dacha, Alexandria. 1927–32. The Peterhof Museum Complex. First publication

The Room for Studies of Tsesarevich Alexis. The Lower Dacha, Alexandria. 1927–32. The Peterhof Museum Complex. First publication

Tsesarevich Alexis in the uniform of the sailor of the yacht Standart. By an unknown sculptor. Russia. 1908–14. Patinated bronze. The Peterhof Museum Complex

The Nursery of Tsesarevich Alexis. The Lower Dacha, Alexandria. 1927–32. In the middle, a small carriage harnessed with toy horses, a portable kitchen with a water barrel and a small car. The Peterhof Museum Complex. First publication

Tsesarevich Alexis in a Russian-Style Costume. Sculptor Amandus Adamson. Russia. 1908–12. Patinated bronze, metal inlay ornament. The Peterhof Museum Complex

*Bookplate of
Tsesarevich Alexis.
By A. E. Felkersam.
1904–10.
The Peterhof
Museum Complex*

*Emperor Nicholas II with his family and retinue
reviewing a parade near the Lower Dacha at Alexandria.
1907–08. The Peterhof Museum Complex*

*Officer's uniform of the Life-Guards of Her Majesty's Uhlan
Regiment. The P. A. Fokin Military Supply Factory, St Petersburg.
1910s. Belonged to Tsesarevich Alexis. Museum of Artillery,
Engineering and Signal Corps, St Petersburg*

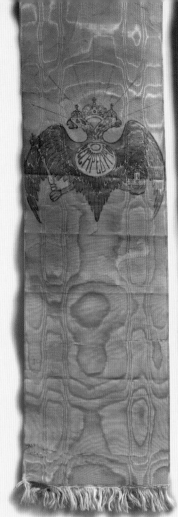

Bands with the monogram of Tsesarevich Alexis. By P. Fiodorov. Russia. Early 20th century. Painted moire. The Peterhof Museum Complex. First publication

The Mosin infantry rifle of the 1891/1910 system, with the bayonet. Calibre 5.08 mm, ²/₃ of the real size, Arms Works, Tula, Russia. 1909. On the butt-end are traces of the monogram: A. N. Belonged to Tsesarevich Alexis. Museum of Artillery, Engineering and Signal Corps, St Petersburg

Parade shako of the Grenadiers Regiment. The Economical Society of the Guards, St Petersburg. 1914–16. Cloth, gold braid, patent leather, metal and silver. On the lining, the golden letter A under the crown. The Peterhof Museum Complex. First publication

Tsesarevich Alexis on a canoe

his children the beloved places with which so many dear memories were connected and as it were parting with them.

After the revolution and the death of the royal family the Lower Dacha was converted into a museum of the history of daily life which existed until 1936. Some art collections from the palace have survived in the stocks of the Peterhof Museum Complex, but the Lower Dacha itself does not exist any more. It was destroyed during the War of 1941–45.

Nowadays, on 12 August, the Heir's birthday, an office for the dead is performed on the ruins every year, and near the Cottage Palace a modest monument produced by the sculptor V. V. Zaiko was installed in 1994.

Valentina Tenikhina

**Medallions with profile relief portraits
of Emperor Nicholas II and Empress
Alexandra Feodorovna. Modelled by A. K. Timus.
The Imperial Porcelain Factory. St Petersburg.
1912 (Alexandra Feodorovna); 1914 (Nicholas II).
Biscuit. The Peterhof Museum Complex**

a swing. I read and worked after a tea. At 8:15 we left our charming home. We had a dinner at Mummy's with aunt Olga, Mitya and Tatyana. At 10:15 we said good-bye to them and left Peterhof."[12]

The family of Nicholas II spent all the subsequent years, until their exile to Tobolsk, at Tsarskoye Selo. The Emperor himself stayed most of his time at the General Headquarters or travelled here and there, often together with the Tsesarevich. Sometimes, on his way to Kronstadt, Nicholas made brief visits to Peterhof.

In the summer of 1915 he visited Peterhof several times with his children. On 5 July he came to Alexandria together with Alexis, Marie and Anastasia. "We were so glad to see the sea! I strolled around Alexandria and bathed in the sea – the temperature of the water was 19°C. Alexis rowed a boat. There were two showers while we were drinking milk and eating fruit in our home. I went around all the rooms."[13]

On 19 July, the day when Germany declared war on Russia, they again were at Peterhof: "At 1:30 I went to Peterhof with Marie, Anastasia, Alexis and Sablin. I made a promenade with him [Sablin] and showed him the interiors of the Cottage and Farm."[14]

Almost a month later, on 16 August 1915, Nicholas II recorded in his Diary: "At 2:15 I went to Peterhof together with Olga, Tatyana, Marie and Alexis, Sablin and V. N. Derevenko. We had a promenade in Alexandria and showed to N. P [Sablin] our church."[15] On 18 August Nicholas II once again went to Kronstadt via Peterhof. These travel turned out to be the last. Nicholas II seemed to have a premonition of that visiting with

[1] *Dnevniki imperatora Nikolaya II*, Moscow, 1991, p. 82.

[2] State Archive of the Russian Federation, fund 490, l. 4, No 1199, fol. 95.

[3] A. A. Mosolov, *Pri dvore poslednego imperatora*, St Peterburg, 1992, p. 234.

[4] *Dnevniki imperatora Nikolaya II*, p. 405.

[5] *Idem*, p. 153.

[6] *Idem*, p. 224

[7] *Idem*, p. 338.

[8] *Idem*, p. 324.

[9] *Idem*, p. 369.

[10] Veliky kniaz' Gavriil Konstantinovich, *V mramornom dvortse. Iz khroniki nashei semyi*, St Petersburg, 1993, p. 97.

[11] *Dnevniki imperatora Nikolaya II*, p. 475.

[12] *Idem*, p. 479.

[13] *Idem*, p. 537.

[14] *Idem*, p. 539.

[15] *Idem*, p. 543.

We moved with a quiet joy to our Standart which glittered and glowed in the sun.

Nicholas II with his family on the yacht Standart [1906–07]. State Archive of the Russian Federation

Grand Duchess Tatyana on the yacht Standart [1906–07]. State Archive of the Russian Federation

Tsesarevich Alexis on the yacht Standart [1908]. State Archive of the Russian Federation

Grand Duchess Marie on the yacht Standart [1906–07]. State Archive of the Russian Federation

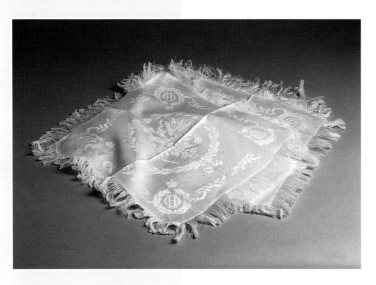

[20] Grand Princess Marie of Russia, *Things I Remember*, London, 1930, p. 43.

The parents divided their children into elder and younger ones. Olga and Tatyana shared a bedroom, the younger girls lived in another room. All slept on similar narrow beds over which hung numerous icons. When the grand princesses were in good health, they had to take cold baths for hardening, with a warm bath in the evening. Their mother chose clothes for them basing on the principle of "two pairs" selecting the colours so that they were similar with the elder and younger ones. But their favourite clothing invariably was a sailor suit, a sign of their attachment to the yacht *Standart*, with which their best days were associated.

Grand Princess Marie Pavlovna (the younger) recollects about the life of the grand princesses at Tsarskoye Selo: "Our apartments at Tsarskoye Selo were in the Great Palace of Catherine II. The Empress would have us come often to the Alexander Palace to play with her daughters. Their nursery apartments occupied an entire wing on the second floor of the Alexander Palace. These rooms, light and spacious, were hung with flowered cretonne and furnished throughout with polished lemonwood. The effect was luxurious, yet peaceful and comfortable… The Emperor's daughters were governed, as we were, by an English head nurse assisted by innumerable Russian nurses and chambermaids… Dmitry [Grand Prince Dmitry Pavlovich] and I spent hours examining our young cousin's toys; one could never tire of them, they were so fine. Especially entertaining for me was the French President's gift to Olga at the time when she was taken with her parents on their first visit to France [in the autumn of 1896]. In a trunk covered with soft leather was a doll with a complete trousseau: dresses, lingerie, hats, slippers, the entire equipment of a dressing-table, all reproduced with remarkable art and fidelity."[20]

Grand Duchess Olga. State Archive of the Russian Federation

*Letter of Grand Duchess Olga
to her mother, Empress
Alexandra Feodorovna.
Sarov. [1903]*

*Letter of Grand Duchess Olga
to her mother, Empress
Alexandra Feodorovna,
on a postcard with
a portrait of Nicholas II.
4 October 1903.*

*State Archive
of the Russian Federation.
First publications*

*Notebook with records
of Grand Duchess Olga. 1906.
State Archive of the Russian
Federation. First publication*

*Notebook with compositions of Grand
Duchess Olga: "The Beautiful Boy", "A Cow
and a Little Hare". 1908. State Archive
of the Russian Federation. First publication*

Vladimir Stasov,
A History of the Book:
Byzantine Enamels by
A. V. Zvenigorodsky,
St Petersburg, 1898.
Published in 150
numbered copies.
Copy No 5 belonged to
Grand Duchess Olga.
The Peterhof Museum
Complex

A sheet from the book:
Vladimir Stasov,
A History of the Book:
Byzantine Enamels by
A. V. Zvenigorodsky.
The Peterhof Museum
Complex

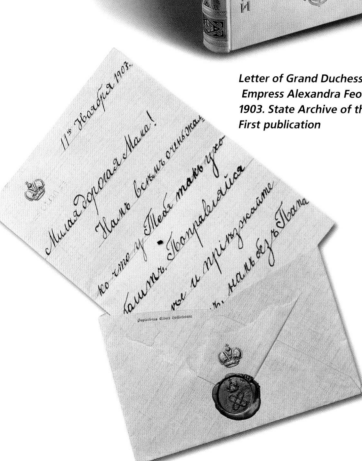

Letter of Grand Duchess Olga to her mother,
Empress Alexandra Feodorovna. 11 November
1903. State Archive of the Russian Federation.
First publication

A drawing by Grand Duchess Olga. Pencil on paper.
Below, the autograph of the grand duchess: O.H. 17/XII 1910.
State Archive of the Russian Federation. First publication

A poem copied by Grand Duchess Olga
with her drawings and congratulations
to her mother, Empress Alexandra
Feodorovna. Tsarskoye Selo. 1910.
Watercolour on paper.
In the lower left corner, the autograph
of the grand duchess: O.H. 1910.
State Archive of the Russian Federation

Letter of Grand Duchess
Olga to her father, Emperor
Nicholas II. Peterhof.
24 June 1909. State Archive
of the Russian Federation.
First publication

A drawing by Grand Duchess Olga.
Watercolour on cardboard.
Below, the autograph
of the grand duchess: O.H. 1913.
State Archive of the Russian
Federation. First publication

A drawing by Grand Duchess Olga.
Watercolour on cardboard. In the
lower right corner, the autograph
of the grand duchess: O.H.
State Archive of the Russian
Federation. First publication

Grand Duchess Olga
by the royal train
near Mogilev on the way
to the General
Headquarters. 1916

The governess of the elder girls was Sophia Ivanovna Tyutcheva, the niece of the great Russian poet Fiodor Tyutchev. The girls affectionately called her "Sovanna". She was an active opponent of Rasputin and that caused her removal from the court in 1912.

The children's life went according to an established daily routine. The whole family gathered for breakfast, followed by lessons. After that they spent some time out of doors. In winter the girls engaged in skating and skiing, in summer they liked to ride a bicycle. Loyal to her habits, the Empress never allowed the daughters to sit idling — after a walk they were busy with handicrafts under her supervision, they learned to weave, to keep household and to draw. At 5 o'clock tea was served after which the girls went out for an evening stroll. By 8 o'clock in the evening all the family gathered at dinner, but if some guests were present, only the elder daughters were admitted and the junior girls dined with maids in the nursery. "The Empress really educated her children herself and she did it wonderfully. It is difficult to imagine more charming, pure and clever girls. She showed her authority only in the case of first necessity, and this did not break the atmosphere of absolute trust which reigned between her and the daughters. She understood the vitality of youth and never restricted them if they played up and laughed. She also liked to be present at their lessons, to discuss with tutors the trend and content of studies," recalled the Empress's maid of honour Baroness Buxhoeveden.[21]

The grand duchesses began training in the subjects taught at the gymnasium rather early. They learned three foreign languages, Russian and literature and playing piano. Although the programme of studies, worked out by Alexandra Feodorovna together with the teacher of French Pierre Gilliard and the teacher of the Russian language and literature Piotr Petrov, was somewhat arbitrary, the grand duchesses received a good education.

[21] S. Buxhoeveden, *The Life and Tragedy of Empress Alexandra Feodorovna*, London–New York, 1928; Quoted in: Nun Nektaria, *Svet nevecherniy. Zhizn' Alexandry Feodorovny Romanovoy, posledney vserossiyskoy imperatritsy*, Moscow, 1996, pp. 51–52.

*Letter of Grand Duchess
Tatyana to her mother,
Empress Alexandra
Feodorovna. Tsarskoye Selo.
31 December 1907. State
Archive of the Russian
Federation. First publication*

*Letter of Grand Duchess
Tatyana to her mother,
Empress Alexandra Feodorovna.
Peterhof. 7 August 1903.
State Archive of the Russian
Federation. First publication*

*A drawing by Grand Duchess
Tatyana. 1913. Oil on canvas.
Below, the autograph of the
grand duchess: T.H. 1913.
State Archive of the Russian
Federation*

Grand Duchess Tatyana.
The Peterhof Museum
Complex

A poem copied by Grand Duchess Olga with her drawings and
congratulations to her mother, Empress Alexandra Feodorovna.
Tsarskoye Selo. 18 April 1910 (?). Watercolour on paper. Below,
the autograph of the grand duchess:
T.H. 1910. State Archive of
the Russian Federation

A congratulation poem copied
by Grand Duchess Tatyana
with her drawings. Tsarskoye
Selo. 25 May 1909.
Watercolour on paper.
State Archive of the Russian
Federation

A drawing by Grand Duchess
Tatyana. 17 December 1910.
Pencil on paper.
The autograph of the grand
duchess, above: мир и покой
[peace and calm]; below:
17 декабря 1910 Т.Н.
[17 December 1910. T. N.].
State Archive of
the Russian Federation.
First publication

**Bookplate of Grand
Duchess Marie.
The Peterhof Museum
Complex**

As contemporaries witnessed, modesty and simplicity became habitual for the grand duchesses. These qualities were educated from an early age and covered the whole daily life of the girls, starting from the Spartan furnishing of their rooms and ending by their dresses. The dresses of the elder girls were readily worn out by their younger sisters. The people around called them by names in the home atmosphere, and when in official occasions they had to name them with full titles, they looked very embarrassed.

Education in the royal family was based on the deep religious grounds of their parents which they succeeded in passing over to their children. According to the Christian teaching, "faith, if it hath not works, is dead." And the girls, together with their mother, engaged much in charities. They dispensed about a half of the modest sum of 15 rubles, which they received every month, as alms to poor people in churches.

Before the beginning of World War I there were rumours about a possible betrothal of one of the grand princesses to prince Carel of Rumania. But the proposal was not made. Perhaps Marie, the Queen of Romania, was afraid to inherit the terrible disease of haemophilia from the Russian imperial family. But another thing is known for sure: the grand princesses would not like to leave Russia.

Numerous reminiscences of contemporaries about the appearances and characters of the girls have reached us. Let us quote some of them. "Olga, the eldest of the Grand-Duchesses, was a girl of ten, very fair, and with sparkling, mischievous eyes and a slightly retroussé nose. She examined me with a look which seemed from the moment to be searching for the weak point in my armour, but there was something so pure and frank about the child that one loved her straight off. The second girl, Tatyana, was eight and a half. She had auburn hair and was prettier than her sister, but gave me the impression of being less transparent, frank, and spontaneous" — these is how Pierre Gilliard first saw the grand duchesses.[22] The girls grew up before him, each had her own character and her own

[22] Pierre Gilliard, *Imperator Nikolai II i yego semya*, Vienna, 1921. Quoted from a reprint edition, Moscow, 1991, p. 18.

Мария
1910

Grand Duchess Marie.
State Archive of
the Russian Federation

*A drawing by Grand Duchess Marie.
15 January 1915. Watercolour
on paper. State Archive of
the Russian Federation.
First publication*

*Album of amateur photographs
devoted to the trips of Nicholas II
and his family to Ilyinskoye
and Nizhni Novgorod and
their life at Peterhof. 1896–97.
State Archive of the Russian
Federation. First publication*

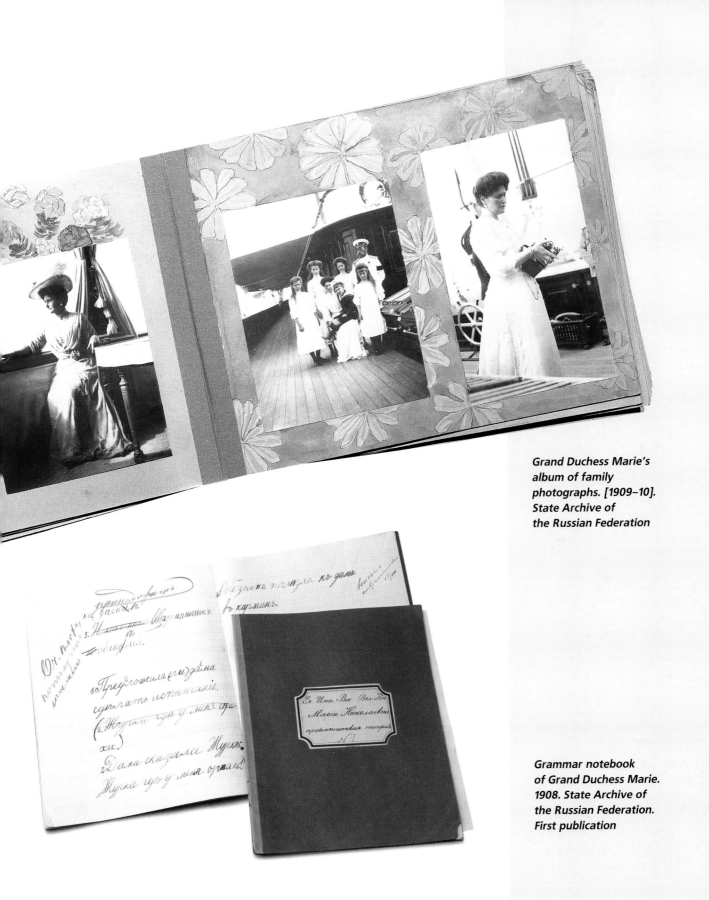

Grand Duchess Marie's
album of family
photographs. [1909–10].
State Archive of
the Russian Federation

Grammar notebook
of Grand Duchess Marie.
1908. State Archive of
the Russian Federation.
First publication

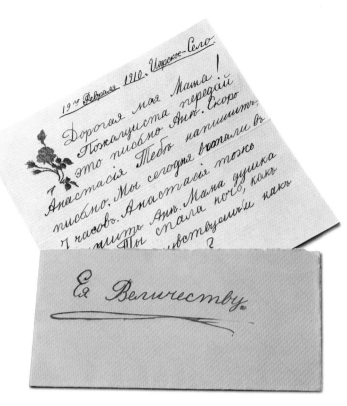

Letter of Grand Duchess Marie to her mother, Empress Alexandra Feodorovna. Tsarskoye Selo. 19 February 1910. State Archive of the Russian Federation. First publication

A drawing by Grand Duchess Marie. 1913. Watercolour on paper. Below, the autograph of the grand duchess: 1913. Мария. Ц.С. State Archive of the Russian Federation. First publication

Grand Duchesses Tatyana and Marie with Pierre Gilliard. Livadia. [1912]

*Diary of Grand
Duchess Marie. 1913.
State Archive of
the Russian Federation.
First publication*

*Diary of Grand Duchess Marie.
1912. State Archive of
the Russian Federation.
First publication*

*A drawing by Grand Duchess
Marie. 1912. Watercolour on
paper. Below, the autograph
of the grand duchess:
M. H. 1912. State Archive of the
Russian Federation*

Bookplate of Grand Duchess Anastasia. The Peterhof Museum Complex

preferences. Having lived with the family for nearly thirteen years, Gilliard wrote about every grand duchess with great warmth: "The eldest, Olga, possessed a remarkably quick brain. She had good reasoning powers as well as initiative, a very independent manner, and a gift for swift and entertaining repartee... She picked up everything extremely quickly, and always managed to give an original turn to what she learned... She had a good deal apart for her lessons... Tatyana Nikolayevna was rather reserved, essentially well balanced, and had a will of her own, though she was less frank and spontaneous than her elder sister. She was not so gifted, either, but this inferiority was compensated by more perseverance and balance. She was very pretty, though she had not quite Olga Nikolayevna's charm. If the Tsarina made any difference between her children, Tatyana Nikolayevna was her favourite... Marie Nikolayevna was a beauty, tall for her age and a picture of glowing health and colour. She had large and beautiful grey eyes. Her tastes were very simple, and with her warm heart she was kindness itself. Her sisters took advantage of somewhat of her good nature, and called her 'fat little bow-vow'. She certainly had the benevolent and somewhat *gauche* devotion of a dog. Anastasia Nikolayevna, on the contrary, was very roguish and almost a wag. She had a very strong sense of honour, and the darts of her wit often found sensitive spots. She was rather an *enfant terrible*, though the fault tended to correct itself with age. She was extremely idle, though with the idleness of a gifted child... In short, the whole charm difficult though it was to define of these four sisters was their extreme simplicity, candour, freshness and instinctive kindness of heart."[23]

With the beginning of the war Olga and Tatyana supervised by the head of the Palace Hospital, Doctor of Medicine Princess Vera Gedroitz, passed a two-month course of nurses. They began to work in the hospital. They assisted, together with their mother, during operations, made bandages and injections and looked after wounded soldiers.

[23] Pierre Gilliard, *Imperator Nikolai II I yego semya*, Vienna, 1921. Quoted from a reprint edition, Moscow, 1991, p. 68–72.

Grand Duchess Anastasia. State Archive of the Russian Federation

Grand Duchess Anastasia

Appliqué work by Grand Duchess Anastasia. Tsarskoye Selo. 23 April 1910. Below and above the passe-partout, the autograph of the grand duchess. State Archive of the Russian Federation

A drawing by Grand Duchess Anastasia presented to her father, Emperor Nicholas II. 9 March 1915. Watercolour on paper. State Archive of the Russian Federation

Крещенскій вечеръ.

Разъ въ крещенскій вечерокъ
        Дѣвушки гадали:
За ворота башмачёкъ,
        Снявъ съ ноги, бросали;
Снѣгъ полали; подъ окномъ
        Слушали; кормили
Счётнымъ курицу зернамъ;
        Ярый воскъ топили;
Въ чашу съ чистою водой
        Клали перстень золотой,
Серги изумрудны;
        Разстилали бѣлый платъ,
И надъ чашей пѣли въ ладъ
        Пѣсенки подблюдны.

                    Анастасія.

Царское-Село.

25 Декабря 1911.

A poem copied by Grand Duchess Anastasia for her mother, Empress Alexandra Feodorovna, and a drawing by the grand duchess. Tsarskoye Selo. 1911. State Archive of the Russian Federation. First publication

24 *Perepiska Nikolaya II I Alexandry,*
Moscow and Leningrad, 1926, vol. 4, p. 146.

They had never been to a ball at the court, but they were already familiar with human pain and suffering, and saw dying people. This could not but influence their characters and views on the world. The Empress complained in a letter to her husband: "Such a complete solitude, the children with all their love still have absolutely different ideas, and they rarely understand my point of view on the things, even the most trifling ones, — they always consider themselves right, and when I tell them how I was educated and how one should be educated, they cannot understand."[24] A usual conflict in the family, where children have grown up and of course one can understand a mother who grieves that her daughters are grown up and that there are no more small children and that she herself becomes older...

OTMA. St Petersburg. 1914.
The Peterhof Museum Complex

Postcard and certificate of the Hospital of Grand Duchesses Marie and Anastasia. Not earlier than 1914. State Archive of the Russian Federation. First publication

Certificate issued to Grand Duchess Olga and confirming that she could work as a nurse. 6 November 1914. State Archive of the Russian Federation

The Hospital of Grand Duchesses Marie and Anastasia. Feodorovsky Settlement. Tsarskoye Selo

A holiday congratulation postcard of Grand Duchesses Olga, Tatyana, Marie and Anastasia to their language and literature teacher Piotr Petrov. 29 June 1915. State Archive of the Russian Federation. First publication

Grand Duchesses Olga and Tatyana as nurses. 1916. State Archive of the Russian Federation

A poem by Nikolai Gumilev (his autograph) dedicated to the birthday of Grand Duchess Anastasia, signed by the officers undergoing cure at the hospital in the Great Palace. Tsarskoye Selo. 5 June 1916. State Archive of the Russian Federation

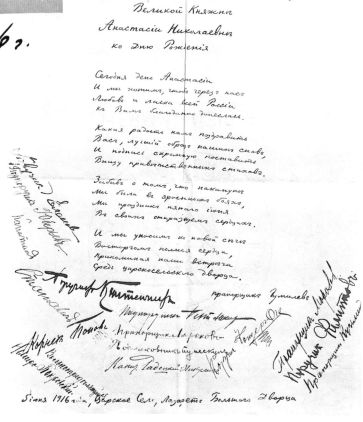

Grand Duchess Tatyana removes plaster cast from the leg of a wounded soldier. Tsarskoye Selo. 1916

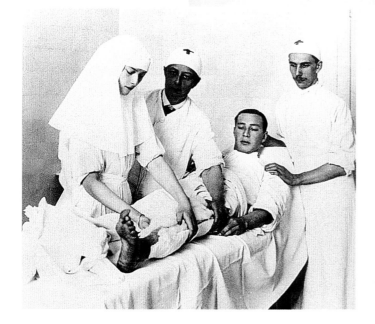

Diary of Grand Duchess Tatyana. 1916. State Archive of the Russian Federation. First publication

Letter of Grand Duchess Marie to her brother, Tsesarevich Alexis. 30 September 1916

Letter of Grand Duchess Marie to her brother, Tsesarevich Alexis. Tsarskoye Selo. 18 August 1916

Letter of Grand Duchess Marie to her brother, Tsesarevich Alexis. 22 September 1915.

State Archive of the Russian Federation. First publications

hile Olga and Tatyana grew up, the younger daughters and Alexis tried more to get in contact with the parents.

The boy's tutor was Pierre Gilliard. A clever and attentive teacher, he soon became intimately associated with the royal family. His advice were attentively listened. Friendly and trusting relations were established between the teacher and his pupil. Gilliard remained loyal to his small pupil even during the days of the Tobolsk exile. At his own risk he went to Ekaterinburg after him, but was not admitted by the authorities to the Ipatyev House.

It must be mentioned that a great role in the education of Alexis, in the formation of his character and habits, was played by simple, half-literate attendants: the boatsman Derevenko, the sailor Nagorny and the nurse Marie Vishniakova. But of course the closest and dearest to Alexis were his parents and sisters. The boy's letters to his father, mother and sisters are sincere and childishly naive. They vividly evoke a homely, solicitous atmosphere surrounding the boy. It is seen in everything starting with the manner the girls used

Tsesarevich Alexis on the yacht The Polar Star. 1907. State Archive of the Russian Federation

Tsesarevich Alexis with a watering-can. [1911].
State Archive of the Russian Federation

addressing their brother: "Our darling small Alexis. In the royal family they liked diminutive names and Alexis was particularly lucky. His father called him in the diary "our little treasure", his mother used an even more affectionate forms: Baby, Little One, Sunbeam, etc. Alexis signed his letters to the parents by the words "The naughty child loving you". The "naughty child" was a sort of parole. It was different in every letter, changing from "naughty child" to 'Impossible', "Irretrievable' or 'Stubborn'. A childish game about which one remembers throughout one's life.

In the autumn of 1915 Nicholas II took his son with him to the General Headquarters. For Alexis it was a great event in his life. For the first time he abandoned his mother and sisters and went with his father to the distinctly man's work — the war. He shared his father's room, where all furnishings were several camp-beds and a number of chairs. From the General Headquarters in Mogilev the Tsarevich went with his father to the disposition of the troops. In memory of his visit to the hospital at Klevan Alexis on 12 October 1915 was awarded the

Tsesarevich Alexis.
[1908]. State Archive
of the Russian Federation

Tsesarevich Alexis. [1910–11].
State Archive of the Russian Federation

Grand Duchess Anastasia
and Tsesarevich Alexis. [1909–10].
State Archive of the Russian Federation

Tsesarevich Alexis with
his attendant Derevenko.
[1910]. State Archive of
the Russian Federation

Medal of St George, 4th degree. In May 1916 he was given the rank of lance-corporal.

In the same 1916 Alexis, imitating his father in everything, began to keep his first diary. He recorded there the events of the day, the names of people he met, almost every day there is the same record: "Studies". On the days of attacks of his malady, he dictated to his tutors or sisters.

Now let us quote Gilliard again: "Alexei Nikolayevich was a clever, sharp and agile boy, in the extreme degree hearty and full of enthusiasm and ardent outbursts. Very simple in his tastes, he extracted no false satisfaction from the fact that he was the Heir — there was nothing he thought about less — and his greatest delight was to play with the two sons of his sailor Derevenko, both of them a little younger than he… He deeply admired his father, deified him and tried to imitate him in everything. Richly endowed, the boy perfectly developed, but was kept back by his infirmity. Each of his crises meant weeks or even months of guarding him, and when the haemorrhage had been particularly heavy, it was followed by a condition of general anaemia which made all hard work impossible for him, sometimes for considerable periods. Only short intervals given by the malady could be used, which made the task of his education, despite the heir's brilliant abilities, very difficult."[25]

Very warm words were written about the boy by A. Mordvinov, the Aide-de-Camps of Emperor Nicholas II, who was close to the family during the last years: "He had

[25] Pierre Gilliard, *Tragicheskaya sud'ba russkoi imperatorskoi familii*, Revel, 1921, pp. 26–27.

A drawing by Tsesarevich Alexis. Watercolour on paper. Above, the autograph of the Tsesarevich: А. Романов. State Archive of the Russian Federation

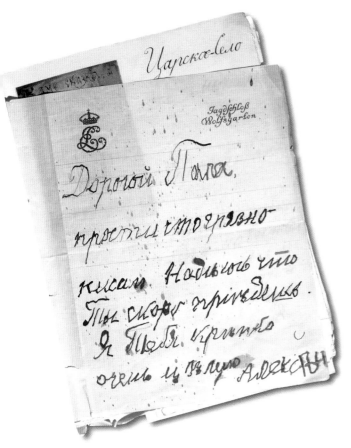

Tsesarevich Alexis's first letter to his father, Emperor Nicholas II. 22 October 1910. State Archive of the Russian Federation

A drawing by Tsesarevich Alexis. Watercolour on paper. Below, the autograph of the Tsesarevich: The aide-de-camp of His Imperial Majesty. State Archive of the Russian Federation

Tsesarevich Alexis's Russian language notebook. 1912–14. State Archive of the Russian Federation. First publication

*Emperor Nicholas II and Tsesarevich Alexis on the bank of
the Dnieper. June 1916. State Archive of the Russian Federation*

*Letter of Tsesarevich Alexis
to his mother, Empress
Alexandra Feodorovna.
Tsarskoye Selo. 1914.
State Archive of
the Russian Federation.
First publication*

[26] A. A. Mordvinov, *Na voenno-pridvornoi sluzhbe* (State Archive of the Russian Federation, fund 5881, l. 2, No 512, p. 42).

what we, Russians, usually call 'a golden heart'. He easily felt an attachment to people, he liked them and tried to do his best to help them, especially when it seemed to him that someone was unjustly was hurt. His love, like with his parents, was based mainly on a pity. Tsarevich Alexei Nikolayevich was an awfully lazy, but very capable boy (I think, he was lazy precisely because he was capable), he easily grasped everything, he was thoughtful and keen over his age. His shyness in the last years, thanks to his frequent stay in the General Headquarters, almost disappeared. Despite his good nature and compassion, he undoubtedly promised to possess a firm and independent character in the future. From his early years he did not very much like to obey and comparatively easily yielded, like his father, only to those arguments which seemed convincing to himself. In the same way as his father and his sisters, he extremely liked the nature of his homeland and all things Russian 'It will be more difficult to cope with him for you than with me', the Sovereign once said to a minister."[26]

A drawing by Tsesarevich Alexis. Watercolour on paper. State Archive of the Russian Federation

Empress Alexandra
Feodorovna and
Tsesarevich Alexis. 1913.
State Archive of
the Russian Federation

Curriculum of Tsesarevich Alexis's studies for 1914–15. State Archive of the Russian Federation. First publication

Game of mosaics presented to Tsesarevich Alexis. State Archive of the Russian Federation. First publication

*Emperor Nicholas II, Empress
Alexandra Feodorovna and
Tsesarevich Alexis in a park.
Mogilev. 1915. The Empress's
first visit to the General
Headquarters. The Peterhof
Museum Complex.
First publication*

*Letter of Tsesarevich
Alexis to his mother,
Empress Alexandra
Feodorovna. The General
Headquarters.
8 November 1916.*

*Letter of Tsesarevich
Alexis to his mother,
Empress Alexandra
Feodorovna. Mogilev.
3 November 1916.*

*State Archive of the
Russian Federation. First
publications*

Mikhail Rundaltsev
*(1871–1935). Portrait
of Tsesarevich Alexis. 1917.
Drypoint. Hermitage,
St Petersburg*

*Tsesarevich Alexis
with the Makarov
brothers.
The General
Headquarters,
Mogilev. 1916.
In the background,
on the left,
the boatsman
Derevenko.
The Peterhof
Museum Complex.
First publication*

Tsesarevich Alexis in a military uniform by a fountain. Eupatoria (?). 1915–16. The Peterhof Museum Complex

Tsesarevich Alexis with his tutors Gibbes, Voyeikov, Petrov and Gilliard at the General Headquarters. 1916. State Archive of the Russian Federation

Menu of a dinner at
the officers' mess of
the Headquarters
on 23 August 1916.
State Archive of the Russian
Federation. First publication

Grand Duchess Olga
and Tsesarevich Alexis.
The Alexander Park.
Tsarskoye Selo. 1917.
State Archive of
the Russian Federation

*On his return
to the Alexander Palace
their father was not
the Emperor of Russia
any more...*

*Tsesarevich Alexis.
The Alexander Park.
Tsarskoye Selo. 1917.
State Archive of
the Russian Federation*

The grandeur and nobility of one's soul is revealed in a disaster, during the minutes of mortal threat, when one must answer to one's own conscience — the more austere judge than all earthly courts.

In the depth of night on 2 March 1917 Emperor Nicholas II signed his abdication. This event was preceded by the days of vague hopes and ominous symptoms of the impending catastrophe. On 22 February Nicholas II went from Petrograd to the General Headquarters to work out military plans. When he left Tsarskoye Selo, his daughters were ill with measles, and a little later Alexis became ill too.

Their father returned thirteen days later to the Alexander Palace not as the Emperor of Russia, but as Colonel Romanov, to whom even a badly educated ensign could not give his hand. And Nicholas's memory still retained the celebration dedicated to the tricentenary of the Romanov dynasty, when thousands of people hurried to express their joy from the contemplation of the Monarch and his children. And now all of a sudden — a confinement to a few rooms of the palace and a guard with fixed bayonets.

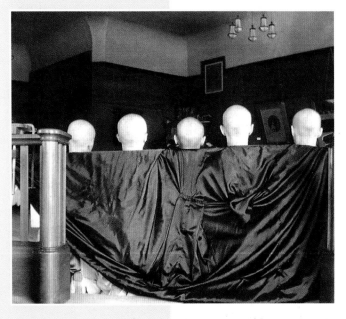

These days marked the beginning of their "road to Calvary". The regime of their captivity at Tsarskoye Selo worked out by Kerensky himself, envisaged strict limitations in the life of the royal family — an isolation from the outer world, a guard during their promenades in the park, prohibition of any contacts and correspondence (letters were allowed only at Kerensky's personal permission).

"In spare time, free from studies, the Empress and her daughters were engaged in sewing something, embroidering or weaving, but they were never idle… During daytime walks all the members of the family, excluding the Empress, were engaged in physical work: they cleaned paths in the park from snow, chopped ice for the cellar, cut dry branches or old trees, storing firewood for the future winter. With the arrival of warm weather the entire family worked on an extensive kitchen-garden, and some officers and soldiers of the guard, who were already accustomed to the royal family and tried to show their attention and disposition, took place in the work together with them. With time the children, on recovering from illnesses, returned to their studies again. Since visits of teachers from the outside was forbidden, the parents organized teaching with the help of those courtiers who shared the confinement with the family."[27]

But the most terrible things were still ahead. The Provisional Government decided to transfer the Romanov family to the remote Siberian town of Tobolsk. In the morning of 1 August 1917 two trains with the imperial family, retinue, servants and soldiers of the Special-Purpose Detachment guarding the prisoners, under the flag of the Japanese Red Cross, started to Tobolsk. They reached the destination on 6 August. The Romanov family was accommodated in a specially prepared mansion which had belonged to the governor of Tobolsk.

[27] "Vospominaniya uchitel'nitsy tsarskikh detei Klavdii Bitner, zapisanniye generalom Dieterichsom", in: M. K. Dieterichs, *Ubiystvo tsarskoi sem'I I chlenov Doma Romanovykh na Urale*, Vladivostok, 1922, pp. 194–195.

Nicholas Alexandrovich Romanov with his son Alexis. Tobolsk. 1918

[28] "Tsarevich Alexis: 'In the afternoon father sawed firewood for a bath and sisters chipped it into splinters', *Moscow News*, No 21, 26 June, 1996.

The routine which formed during the life under arrest at Tsarskoye Selo was followed in Tobolsk too. At 8:45 morning tea was served. Then lessons began. At one o'clock the entire family gathered for lunch. In the evening, when early dusk covered the town, the children liked to stand by the windows watching passers-by. Alexis recorded during one of such evenings: "The whole evening passed as yesterday and was no less boring."[28] To make their life more rich in content, the parents studied much with their children, read aloud Russian classics of literature, staged home performances in English and French.

After the October Revolution of 1917, the regime of the family's confinement changed. In April 1918 the authorities made up a decision to transfer the royal family from Tobolsk to Ekaterinburg, a bulwark of the Bolshevik power in the Urals. On 17 April Nicholas, Alexandra and the Grand Duchess Marie were brought to Ekaterinburg. The children left at Tobolsk missed them greatly. As soon as Alexis recovered after a long period of pain in his leg, they were also sent to Ekaterinburg.

Two months were left until Alexis's birthday. He mainly stayed in bed, but sometimes he was carried out to breath fresh air. The sisters were already thinking about a present to their dear brother. Nicholas and Alexandra looked more quiet in this last period, when the entire family was together.

Olga Barkovets

*Emperor Nicholas II
and Empress Alexandra
Feodorovna. 1917.
State Archive of
the Russian Federation*

Life turned out to be more terrible than any forecasts. When the family was ordered to move to the new place, Nicholas carried his son in his arms. It was their road to death. During the night of 17 July 1918 the Bolsheviks with medieval cruelty shot in the basement of the Ipatyev House the last Russian Emperor Nicholas II, his wife Alexandra Feodorovna and their children —

OTMA plus Alexis.

When I shall die, put up a small stone monument in the park to me.

*Alexis,
Spala, 1912*